The Book of

JOY

Journal

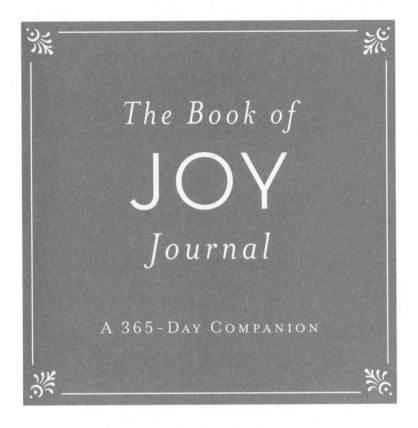

The Book of

JOY

Journal

A 365-DAY COMPANION

HIS HOLINESS THE DALAI LAMA
AND ARCHBISHOP DESMOND TUTU

WITH DOUGLAS ABRAMS

AVERY
an imprint of Penguin Random House
New York

AVERY

an imprint of Penguin Random House LLC
375 Hudson Street
New York, New York 10014

Most Avery books are available at special quantity discounts for bulk purchase for sales promotions, premiums, fund-raising, and educational needs. Special books or book excerpts also can be created to fit specific needs. For details, write SpecialMarkets@penguinrandomhouse.com.

ISBN 9780525534822

Printed in the United States of America
1   3   5   7   9   10   8   6   4   2

BOOK DESIGN BY LUCIA BERNARD

The Book of

JOY

Journal

❧ AN INVITATION TO A YEAR OF JOY ☙

We hope this small book will be an invitation to more joy
and more happiness.

Lasting happiness cannot be found in pursuit of any goal
or achievement. It does not reside in fortune or fame. It
resides only in the human mind and heart, and it is here
that we hope you will find it.

You don't need to believe us. Indeed, nothing we say
should be taken as an article of faith. We hope you will
discover whether what is included here is true by applying it
in your own life.

Every day is a new opportunity to begin again.

—His Holiness the Dalai Lama and Archbishop Desmond Tutu,
The Book of Joy

You are made for perfection, but you
are not yet perfect. You are a
masterpiece in the making.

—ARCHBISHOP DESMOND TUTU

1

2

3

4

5

6

7

8

9

10

11

12

13

14

15

16

We have perceptions about our experience, and we judge them: "This is good." "This is bad." "This is neutral. . . ." Then we have responses: fear, frustration, anger. We realize that these are just different aspects of mind. They are not the actual reality.

—HIS HOLINESS THE DALAI LAMA

17

18

19

20

21

22

23

24

25

26

29

30

31

32

You know, if you did not feel fear
when you saw a lion over there and
you just walked merrily by, in next to
no time there would be no you. . . .
The problem is when the fear is
exaggerated or when it is provoked by
something that is really quite
insignificant.

—ARCHBISHOP DESMOND TUTU

33

34

35

36

37

38

39

40

41

42

45

46

47

48

Stress and anxiety often come from
too much expectation and too much
ambition. . . . Then, when we don't
fulfill that expectation or achieve that
ambition, we experience frustration.

—HIS HOLINESS THE DALAI LAMA

49

50

53

54

59

60

61

62

To hold down emotions in a controlled environment, as it were, is not wise. I would say go ahead and even maybe shout out your sadness and pain. This can bring you back to normal. It's locking them up and pretending that they are not there that causes them to fester and become a wound.

—ARCHBISHOP DESMOND TUTU

65

66

69

70

73

74

75

76

77

78

The way through the sadness and grief that comes from great loss is to use it as motivation and to generate a deeper sense of purpose.

—HIS HOLINESS THE DALAI LAMA

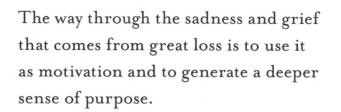

85

86

88

89

90

93

94

95

96

Despair can come from deep grief, but it can also be a defense against the risks of bitter disappointment and shattering heartbreak. Resignation and cynicism are easier, more self-soothing postures that do not require the raw vulnerability and tragic risk of hope.

—ARCHBISHOP DESMOND TUTU

97

98

99

100

101

102

105

106

109

110

111

112

If you live with fear and consider yourself as something special, then automatically, emotionally, you are distanced from others. You then create the basis for feelings of alienation from others and loneliness.

—HIS HOLINESS THE DALAI LAMA

113

114

117

118

125

126

It is not that you wake up in the morning and you say, Now, I'm going to be envious. It just rises spontaneously. . . . I mean, you get up, and you're trying to be a good person and that guy goes past yet again, for the third time this week, in his Mercedes-Benz. . . .

—ARCHBISHOP DESMOND TUTU

129

130

133

134

135

136

137

138

141

142

143

144

. . . once a person develops a strong negative emotion, like anger or jealousy, it is very difficult to counter it at that moment. So the best thing is to cultivate your mind through practice so that you can learn to prevent it from arising in the first place.

—HIS HOLINESS THE DALAI LAMA

145

146

149

150

153

154

157

158

It is wonderful. I mean, imagine if we didn't die. Our poor world would not be able to carry the burden. It's not able to carry the burden of seven billion as it is. I mean, I have had a beginning, I've had a middle, and I'll have an end. There is a lovely symmetry about it.

—ARCHBISHOP DESMOND TUTU

161

162

165

166

167

168

169

170

173

174

I thought of Shantideva's somewhat stern advice: If there is a way to overcome the situation, then instead of feeling too much sadness, too much fear, or too much anger, make an effort to change the situation. If there's nothing you can do to overcome the situation, then there is no need for fear or sadness or anger.

—HIS HOLINESS THE DALAI LAMA

177

178

181

182

185

186

187

188

189

190

If you set out and say, I want to be happy, clenching your teeth with determination, this is the quickest way of missing the bus.

—ARCHBISHOP DESMOND TUTU

197

198

201

202

205

206

208

We must look at any given situation or problem from the front and from the back, from the sides, and from the top and the bottom—so from at least six different angles. This allows us to take a more complete and holistic view of reality and, if we do, our response will be more constructive.

—HIS HOLINESS THE DALAI LAMA

209

210

211

212

213

214

217

218

221

222

The very fact of not thinking about your own frustration and pain does something. I don't know why. But it will make you feel much better.

—ARCHBISHOP DESMOND TUTU

225

226

227

228

229

230

231

232

237

238

239

240

I used to get nervous when I was young and had to give some formal teachings, because I was not thinking that we are all same, I would experience anxiety. I would forget that I'm just talking as a human being to fellow human beings. I would think of myself as something special, and that kind of thinking would make me feel isolated.

—HIS HOLINESS THE DALAI LAMA

245

246

248

249

250

251

 252

253

254

Sometimes we confuse humility with timidity . . . Humility is the recognition that your gifts are from God, and this lets you sit relatively loosely to those gifts. Humility allows us to celebrate the gifts of others, but it does not mean you have to deny your own gifts or shrink from using them.

—ARCHBISHOP DESMOND TUTU

257

258

259

260

261

262

263

264

269

270

So many people . . . seem to struggle with being kind to themselves. This is really sad. You see, if you don't have genuine love and kindness toward yourself, how can you extend these to others?

—HIS HOLINESS THE DALAI LAMA

273

274

277

278

280

281

282

285

286

287

288

I have been helped by my wife, Leah, who was very—is very—good at keeping me humble. Once, we were driving, and I noticed that she was a little smugger than she normally is. And then when I looked again at the car in front of us, I saw a bumper sticker that said: "Any woman who wants to be equal to a man has no ambition."

—ARCHBISHOP DESMOND TUTU

289

290

293

294

295

296

297

298

299

300

301

302

You cannot control your neighbor, but you do have some control over your thoughts and feelings. Instead of anger, instead of hatred, instead of fear, you can cultivate compassion for them, you can cultivate kindness toward them, you can cultivate warm-heartedness toward them.

—HIS HOLINESS THE DALAI LAMA

305

306

307

308

309

310

313

314

317

318

320

In our view also those people who are committing atrocities, including murder, are creating karma that brings very serious negative consequences. So there are many reasons to feel a sense of real concern for their well-being.

—ARCHBISHOP DESMOND TUTU

321

322

325

326

329

330

333

334

336

Where the wrong action is concerned, it may be necessary to take appropriate counteraction to stop it. Toward the actor, or the person, however, you can choose not to develop anger and hatred.

—HIS HOLINESS THE DALAI LAMA

337

338

339

340

341

342

343

344

345

346

349

350

You can't flourish without other
human beings. They give you things
that you cannot give yourself, no
matter how much money you have.
And so we speak of Ubuntu. A person
is a person through other persons.

—ARCHBISHOP DESMOND TUTU

353

354

355

356

357

358

361

362

363

364

365

So all of us, spiritual brothers and sisters, have a special responsibility, have a special role to make clear that the ultimate source of a meaningful life is within ourselves. If you live in this way, until your last breath comes you will be a happy, happy person. That's the goal of human life—to live with joy and purpose.

—HIS HOLINESS THE DALAI LAMA

NOTES

NOTES